TO TUMBLEDOWN
AND BEYOND

The Robert Osborn Story

Researched and collated

By

Betty Elmer

This book is dedicated by Robert Osborn to the memory of his father David Osborn. Scots Guards (1940-1946)

With many thanks to good friends

Ela Watts – Publisher

Anne Brooks – Secretarial Services

Table of Contents

Preface

To Tumbledown and Beyond

A Job That Goes With A Bang!

Epilogue

Summary

PREFACE

TO TUMBLEDOWN AND BEYOND is Robert Osborn's verbatim account of his army life. It was researched and collated by Betty Elmer who is a local broadcaster and published author. Betty lives in Grantham, an historic market town situated in rural Lincolnshire in Eastern England. Former Scots Guards Sergeant Robert Osborn is presently the Assistant Curator of The Queen's Royal Lancers and Nottinghamshire Yeomanry Museum.

TO TUMBLEDOWN AND BEYOND

I was born on the 10th May 1961 in St Thomas' Hospital in Lambeth.

When I was about two and a half we moved up to Belvoir (pronounced Beever) and I went to school in the local Bottesford Primary School, then to Belvoir High School. When I was at school and as a young child, looking back, I must have been an absolute horror. Although we didn't realise it at the time I had severe hearing problems and I was a guinea pig for an operation carried out at Grantham Hospital by Mr Port, a senior surgeon. I had this op five times on one ear and six on the other. So it was eleven in total and this is now a standard operation for children and is the insertion of a grommet. This obviously worked because when I did go to join the Army I had a little bit of a worry on the hearing side, but I got in with A1 hearing. Once I got to fourteen I moved on to the King Edward VII Grammar School at Melton Mowbray.

We were getting round to the exams and had a few days when I wasn't at school, so I came into Grantham when it started to chuck it down with rain. I decided to pop into the Army Recruiting Centre. Went in, got home and told Mum and Dad that I wasn't going back to school.

Dad said. "Well, if you are not going back to school then you are getting a job."

I said. "Don't need to, I've already got one."

"Oh, what's that?"

I said. "I've joined the Army."

That was in April 1977. I joined on August 8th that year and Mum and Dad had to go and get my exam results because I was already in training at the time. I went through the training first at Shorncliffe, then at the Guards Depot at

Pirbright, passing out at Pirbright. I was then posted to the 2nd Battalion the Scots Guards. We were in Munster in Germany at the time. We were over there for six to eight months before we came back to the UK.

Our first big parade, it was the first time that both battalions had been together in London for something like one hundred and odd years and we had a big regimental review on Horse Guards. Went through a round of public duties and in 1980 we went on tour of West Belfast, that was May 1980. We came back from there and then as we got into 1982 April 2nd we heard that the Falklands had been invaded. We thought. "We won't be involved with that." But basically the next day we were told. "Yes, we are!"

In the February of 1982 before the Falklands kicked off I had been having problems with the cartilage in the joint of my jaw and the joint was taken apart and then rebuilt. I wasn't meant to fire weapons for six months. It just shows how much notice I take because within six weeks I was back firing weapons and preparing to go to the Falklands.

We were then trying to pull together all the equipment we would need and they decided to send the battalion along with the Welsh Guards and the 1st/7th Duke of Edinburgh's Own Gurkha Rifles to do some training in an area that was similar to the Falklands. The only thing was it must have been one of the hottest late Easters there had been for a while, so although the terrain was similar the weather most certainly was not. That was down in the Brecon Beacons where we managed to set a couple of hillsides on fire during the training.

When we came back from there we had a couple of days leave in which time I had my 21st birthday, two days early, as we had to report back to Chelsea on my 21st and two days later we sailed for the Falklands from Southampton on the QE2.

Working our way south, most of the time we were saying "we're not going to get there – we're not going to be involved, it's going to be over before we get there."

On the way to the Falklands on the QE2 there was an in-house radio station and it probably reflects on the squaddies sense of humour that the top three tunes requested, in reverse order were:

3. The Scotland World Cup Squad.

2.   The Dawn Patrol (from the Jungle Book)

1. I want to be a Man Cub (Jungle Book).

On the way down there one of the broadcasts from the BBC World Service stated that Argentina had announced that they had sunk H.M.S. Dolphin which I found extremely amusing and started to laugh.   A few of the boys weren't too happy about this until I pointed out that H.M.S. Dolphin is what is known as a stone frigate because basically it is the shore station at Portsmouth.   If they had managed to hit that from the South Atlantic then we were in trouble.

Eventually, via Freetown in Sierra Leone, we pulled into Grytviken in South Georgia, crossed deck onto the Canberra and then three days later we sailed into Falklands Sound and our first landing was at San Carlos. After a few days in San Carlos we boarded Landing Ship Intrepid to sail round to just north of Lively Island, followed by a two hour trip in landing craft into Bluff Cove, well that was the idea.

The Navy dropped us well south of Lively Island and we had an eight hour run into Bluff in open landing craft, during which our own Navy fired at us, but we managed to dodge them.

We arrived in Bluff Cove on June 6th the day before the 1st Battalion The Welsh Guards came round from San Carlos in The Galahad. Although Bluff Cove is within the same inlet of water as Fitzroy, it is about fifteen miles to the north by land; there is a small settlement at each inlet.   Once at Bluff Cove we were just getting ourselves sorted out when we got an air raid warning Red.   The Welsh Guards had come round on Galahad which was still there in the waters just off Fitzroy and The Galahad was hit. A lot of the Welsh lads with whom I'd been through training were on the ship.

It is surprising you remember the funny anecdotes that happened when we were at Bluff Cove. We were told to get under cover and get a brew. Most of the cover had been taken and one of the only places left was the pigsty. I asked the farmer if we could use it. So myself and a young lad who was with us ended up in the shelter of this pigsty. Mr Kilmartin, the farmer, said the piglets would probably have a look at us then go to the other end while the mother might fuss around a bit. As it was the mother took one smell of us lot and shifted to the other end.   We spent the whole time trying to keep the piglets out and stopping them from actually taking our drink.

There were a few comments afterwards like "wherever we were going to be we had to be downwind from everybody else."

What a way to go to war, ending up having a brew in a pigsty.

On 13th June we moved by helicopter to our Forming Up Area (FUA) on Goat Ridge prior to our attack on Mount Tumbledown. Five minutes after we were supposed to have crossed the Start Line (SL) at midnight I was still sitting on it with my back to Tumbledown eating a tin of tuna with hard tack biscuits. We started to advance onto Mount Tumbledown which is the highest point in the final ring of mountains around Port Stanley.

My own Company was Left Flank and we spent the next eight hours in contact with the enemy who were the 5th Battalion Infantry Marine and not a conscript unit as a lot were down in the Falklands, but this was one of their regular units.

After Left Flank had completed its part of the attack we were detailed to act as a security screen to get some of the wounded back to the Regimental Aid Post. This was on Goat Ridge. As we were going back, after a short distance we stopped and swapped places with the stretcher bearers becoming the screen and the screen actually carrying the stretchers. Five seconds after we restarted we were hit by mortar fire. The outcome of this was that from two on stretchers and one walking wounded we finished up with two dead and twelve or thirteen were injured. The person I swapped with, Guardsman David Malcolmson was killed outright, and my left leg was badly injured. At the time I wasn't really fussed about it. I thought it was a broken ankle, but I was concerned as I felt a piece of shrapnel go into my thigh.

Another party from Left Flank returning from the Regimental Aid Post was the first to reach us.

My first question was: "Where have my glasses gone?"

They carried those of us who were unable to walk back to the RAP from where I was helicoptered first to Fitzroy field hospital then to Ajax Bay. From Goat Ridge to Fitzroy my legs were sticking out of the side of the helicopter, a flapping tarpaulin covering then. It b***** well hurt and using unprintable language I told the crewman so when we landed.

Some of us went straight from Fitzroy to Ajax Bay, the red and green life machine with Rick Jolly and his crew. That is where I had my first operation and it was there we heard that the Argentinians were in the process of surrendering.

From Ajax Bay I was helicoptered out to "Mother Hen", the Hospital Ship Uganda. Whilst being carried down to "Sea View" Ward I scrounged a packet of ciggies off a young P&O crew member (nicknamed Storm).

Once on "Sea View", the high dependency ward at the stern of the ship, I met with Staff Nurse (LNN) Diane Aldwinckle, and lost my last piece of clothing (i.e. my underpants).

On the sixth day on board Surgeon Lieutenant Warner came to see me and explained the full extent of my injuries, and that I was going to lose the leg. Two days later (five years to the day I had left school) my left leg was amputated. A quarter past three on the 22nd June.

I was surprised that the medical staff had tried to save my leg, but in the long run, for me anyway, it helped as it gave me some time to adjust to everything. I remember signing the consent form with Doctor Bull and Theatre Sister Nicci Pugh whilst on the operating table.

They were both very kind and seemed to care about every patient individually which is quite something considering the job they were doing and the rate of casualties going through their operating theatres at the time.

Some days later the journey back to the UK started by being transferred onto the Survey (Ambulance) Ship Hydra for a three day journey up to Montevideo. I was one of the very few who managed to sneak crutches off the Uganda and I still have them.

From the port in Montevideo we were transported individually to The International Airport to fly back to the UK on a VC10 via Ascension. The road from the port to the Airport was the worse I had and still have ever travelled on. The two man crew of the ambulance I was in were comedians (i.e. lunatics). Whilst waiting to be loaded onto the VC10 they spotted an Argentinian civil aircraft taxiing and asked if I fancied having a shot at it.

Jokingly, I said "yes, why not."

So they called over a Uruguayan soldier to ask if I could borrow his gun. His answer was "yes", but it would not be any good as he didn't have any ammunition ......

The VC10 landed at Brize Norton from where we were transferred to RAF Wroughton for post flight medicals. After we had all been checked then, obviously from different units, we were all broken up. Marines went to either Stonehouse at Plymouth or Hasler at Portsmouth. Parachute Regiment members and others went to the Cambridge Military Hospital at Aldershot.

Scots and Welsh Guards ended up at the Queen Elizabeth Military Hospital (QEMH) at Woolwich. The first time my dressing was changed I had to have a pre-med and go to theatre. I was not impressed especially when told I had to have nil by mouth eight hours prior. On the Hospital Ship Uganda it was done on the ward.

For my first sick leave I arrived home to a big welcome from the village. It was a total surprise. I told my Dad I would get him back for not telling me about it. It took me nine years but I got him back on his 70th.

I was offered rehabilitation at Chessington or Headley Court but refused it. While I was at Queen Mary's University Hospital at Roehampton I was measured for my first leg. This was before my "Welcome Home" celebrations. Then there were numerous trips back down to Woolwich limb fitting centre.

It was during this time that a lass in the village, who had just come back from the Paralympics in Arnhem, took me over to the disabled sports club at Nottingham, the Nottingham Panthers. I started doing sports and took part in my first competition and that was one hundred and forty one days after my original injury. It was the East Midlands Super Stars and I finished second. That started me off doing sports and since then I've been to seven World Championships in eight different sports. I have amassed just under four and a half thousand podium finishes, two hundred and two at International level. I still compete even now. I threw myself into disabled sport, rising from being a complete novice up to the honour of captaining the disabled National shooting team at the World Championships. I didn't restrict myself to disabled sports; I also competed for the Regular Army team and was selected to represent Scotland as an "able bodied competitor" at a number of International events. Along with my numerous sporting activities as a competitor, I also qualified as an official and/or coach in many of them as well.

Somehow I also found time to qualify as a driver and I obtained my pilot's licence.

During the same year, whilst on attachment to the Jungle Warfare Training Centre in Australia, I gained my speedboat drivers licence. My first International was the 1986 World Championships in Hungary.

In 1991 at the Inaugural Disabled Ex-Service Championships I won 3 gold, 2 silver and a bronze. In the same year I got into the Army Shooting Squad. In 2001 I got into the Able-Bodied National Squad. I have competed in 272 County,

76 Regional, 166 National and 60 International Championships in the following events:- athletics, swimming, air weapons, road racing, volleyball, table tennis, small and full bore pistol, dragon boat racing, cross bow, water polo, gallery rifle, bowls, weight lifting, slalom, power lifting, archery, small bore, target, full bore, classic and light weight sports rifle.

I gained 1146 County (648 gold), 211 Regional (87 gold), 689 National (361 gold), 204 International medals (95 gold) and 4332 medals overall (1423 gold).

So you can see I'm quite a competitive bloke. I mention this because once I knew the leg had to go; I had to face up to a new and different way of life. I have just carried on working hard and enjoying all these sports and new friends I've made. Some of the things I might never have got to do if it hadn't been for the injury, which is a funny way of looking at it, but it's true.

Somehow, I also furthered my education attaining degrees with both Arizona State and Penn State Universities.

In 1988 I was awarded a Douglas Bader Flying Scholarship.

Before I lost my leg I would walk or run everywhere and had only driven Military vehicles off-road. I got my first car via South Atlantic Fund/Regiment/Local Dealer, then given a four and a half day, 1000 mile driving course followed by passing my test.

I stayed in the Army completing just short of 24 years.

Eighteen months after losing my leg I was posted to the Depot to run the swimming pool (not bad, as before I lost my leg I couldn't swim), in 1986 I left the Depot and joined B Coy of the 1st Battalion as storeman for six months, before taking over the Map & Training stores for the Battalion.

When the Battalion moved to Cyprus I was attached to HQ Coy of the 1st

Battalion Irish Guards to run the Pool & Gymnasium in Chelsea, where I remained for the next 30 months, being attached to the holding unit (i.e. 2nd Battalion Coldstream Guards & 238 (London) Signal Squadron RS).

In May 1990, although on the held strength of the holding unit at Chelsea Barracks (1st Battalion Irish Guards, 238 (London) Signal Squadron RS & 7 (PDI) Coy Coldstream Guards) and after Chelsea Barracks closed the holding unit at Woolwich (16 (Air Defence Regiment Royal Artillery & Woolwich Garrison), I finally returned to the held strength of the 1st Battalion Scots Guards at Wellington Barracks in May 2000. I took over the running of Burton Court (the District Sports Grounds) for G3 PAT Headquarters London District, until May 10th 2001 when I completed my 22 years Colour Service.

I'm a BLESMA (British Limbless Ex-Service Men's Association) member and was on the first South Atlantic Medal

Association (SAMA82) return Pilgrimage to the Falkland Islands in 2002. In 2007 I made my own way back for the 25th Anniversary Pilgrimage, staying with Bill and Clara McKay on both occasions. Bill, Clara and their family have become very good friends; they open their house and their hearts to me. It is wonderful how kind everyone is in The Islands to returning veterans. I hope to get back to the Falklands again in the near future.

After the big Commemorations of the 25th Anniversary of the Falklands War in and around London I heard through BLESMA of the first Hospital Ship Uganda Reunion which was being held on board a cruise ship in Southampton in April 2008. This was the first time anyone from the Hospital Ship had met and all the former patients were included. Amazing! I signed up straight away. I wanted to meet up with all the Navy medical teams who had helped me after my injuries. It was a brilliant weekend. People had travelled from all over the UK and abroad. We all based ourselves at a nearby

Premier Inn and were on board Aurora by 10am on the Sunday morning. There were nearly 200 of us altogether. I especially wanted to meet and talk with Di Aldwinckle, who was the Staff nurse on Sea View Ward, who had been so good to me, and Sister Nicci Pugh, who I knew by then, had assisted at my operation when the leg was amputated. I sat with Sister Margaret Kerr, the other Theatre Sister on board Uganda and Chief Jim Lacey for lunch, and also spent time with Doc Beeley and Doc Bull. They were all very kind and professional, and didn't mind talking about my treatment at all. I'm going to keep in touch with all the group now, as I think they did a fantastic job for us all down there, and no-one ever seems to mention them. I like their new name, which is HUGS 2009, the letters stand for Hospital Ship Uganda. Anyway that's what nurses do a lot of, and they're a great crowd of lassies (and some gents, of course!)

During the whole time I was on the Hospital Ship in 1982, I got the best treatment and most importantly care from the Navy Medical team that was possible, especially members of "The Fearless Forty".

A Big Thank You to All

"HUGS"

You'll always be special to me.

I must mention the "Fearless Forty". These were the first junior female ratings to serve on board a ship. They were referred to as The "QUARNS" which stands for Queen Alexandra's Royal Nurses Service. They were naval party 1830 on the hospital ship. They decided to hold a reunion and it was called HSUR, Hospital Ship Uganda Reunion.

They invited some of us who had been wounded and had been on board Uganda to join them. A few of us sat around and weren't impressed with the acronym they were using. Playing with letters we came up with HUGS, Hospital Ship Uganda Group. We thought that HUGS was most appropriate as that is what nurses give.

I'm still in contact with them and a few of us who had been wounded persuaded one of the nursing sisters who had been a nursing sister on the hospital ship to write the story of the Uganda during that time. This she did. Her comment was: "I don't know why I've bothered because nobody is going to read it."

It is now in its fifth reprint as well as an electronic version and Nicci now spends her time going round giving talks not only on the Uganda but also hospital ships through the ages.

The book that was written by Nicci Pugh was called "White Ship, Red Crosses" and was published by Melrose Publishing.

What Nicci did apart from telling the story about the doctors, nurses and stretcher bearers who were on the Uganda, she got a number of us who were wounded to write down a piece of how we ended up in the services, arrived down in the Falklands, our injuries, our time on the Uganda and what we have done since. She then separated these into sections and incorporated within her book.

After finishing in the Army in 2001, because I couldn't get an extension to my service, I spent the first six months acting as a full time carer to my Dad, who had just been diagnosed with Parkinson's disease. After his condition stabilized I worked part time as a guide at a stately home, before being offered the job I now hold as Assistant Curator in the Queen's Royal Lancers Regimental Museum. I was also appointed as The Cannon Master to His Grace the Duke of Rutland. This is an honorary position, of which I am extremely proud. The cannons are original 18th Century cannons and I fire them at Belvoir Castle at The Duke's request for events, anniversaries etc. On June 14th 2008 we had a special seven cannon firing for the Liberation of the Falkland Islands 26th Anniversary and we are all hoping very much His Grace will allow this to continue up to the 30th Anniversary.

A JOB THAT GOES WITH A BANG!

On May 23rd 2004 I took up the appointment of Cannon Master to His Grace the Duke of Rutland. As I have now passed the 11th Anniversary it's an appropriate time to look back over this time.

I have chalked up quite a tally since that first firing; the 12th December 2015 will be the 183rd occasion on which I have fired the cannons using a 1/3 of a ton of black powder in the process, firing 1166 cannons in total.

Of that 183, 140 have been for weddings, 50 Battle Honours have been commemorated (Tumbledown every year since the 24th (2006) anniversary).

On the 25th Anniversary of Tumbledown, I was joined by His Grace, The Castle Chaplain (Reverend Stuart Foster) and a local piper (Bill James).

When firing the cannons for weddings, it is usually in uniform (either Tunic or Greatcoat Order depending on the time of year), on these occasions I request a donation for charity, the best being received from Mr and Mrs Gareth Gates (which ended up in the Colonel's Fund and I got my picture in OK Magazine (well alright only because Holly Willoughby was in the picture "but it still counts"). To-date I have raised £10,850 for 80 different charities (no charity benefitting more than once in a year).

(Photo Robert Osborn and Holly Willoughby)

Two cannon fires have been filmed, successfully (eventually), the first being an advert for Stilton Cheese to be shown in Australia, (writing off one of their cameras in the process – their own fault having insisted on putting it 20 feet away directly in front of the cannon), the other occasion was for the Final of Ukrainian TV's version of The Batchelor (have you ever tried explaining to a Ukrainian producer who doesn't understand English or their own language spoken by their own translator, why they can't stand in front of a cannon when it's fired. Eventually I gave up trying and just fired the cannon they were standing next to. She and the whole crew shifted well out of the way after that, and just to really annoy her, whilst waiting for them to get their act together, I turned my car stereo on and had the RSDG Pipes & Drums CD "Parallel Tracks" belting out "The Gael" at full blast (unfortunately I didn't have an SG CD in the car at the time). Apparently she wasn't too keen on the Pipes either. The filming eventually went off OK and even after upsetting her plans, she paid up!

I have set myself a target of raising £25k, 2000 cannons fired and having marked all of the Regiments Battle Honours before the 25th Anniversary (well I'll have turned 68 by then and will be looking at retiring).

A lot of the weddings prefer the cannons to be fired at night, although more challenging for me than in daylight (ever tried finding a cannon in the dark), it is a more spectacular event.

I think you'll agree I definitely get a bang out of this job!

All of the above is in addition to the "Day Job" as Assistant Curator of the QRL&NY

Museum (that seems to involve firing cannons as well).

Anyone finding themselves in the area of Thoresby Courtyard, North Nottinghamshire NG22 9EP are welcome to visit (it's free to enter). Opening times are 10:30 till 16:00 Wednesday to Sunday and Bank Holidays, 1st March to 30th November.

EPILOGUE

After completing his Colour Service he went to work for the 11th Duke of Rutland in a variety of roles (guide, deputy head guide, security, emergency relief (entrance and shop), chauffeur, public relations distribution, but mainly as the Honorary Quartermaster Sergeant and Armourer for the Belvoir Castle Company of the Leicestershire Volunteers and first as the deputy Carillion Master and eventually as the Cannon Master for the Castle; a position he held for several years.

Having an in-depth knowledge of military history, his special interests include Firearms, Battle Honours and Battlefield cartography.

In April 2004 he was appointed as the assistant curator of The Queens Royal Lancers Museum (becoming the "In-House" Specialist on Firearms, Battlefield Cartography and Battles Nomclature), first at Belvoir and then, when it closed, at Lancer House for 4 years before it re-opened at Thoresby Courtyard for another 7 years, then on the QRL & 9th/12th Lancers amalgamation in May 2015 (forming The Royal Lancers) taking up the same post.

During his time with the Lancers he helped compile a number of books (although not credited); A Pictorial History of the 16th & 17th Lancers for their 250th Anniversary, one of which was presented to the QRL's Colonel in Chief Her Majesty Queen Elizabeth II, A short History of the QRL (and its Antecedent Regiments).

He also contributed to Nicci Pugh's "White Ship, Red Crosses" (the story of HMHS Uganda in the Falklands).

SUMMARY

Falklands made Robert a survivor.

Every war has its victims, but it also has its survivors.

One such survivor is Falkland's veteran and former Scots Guardsman, Robert "Ossie" Osborn, who grew up in Belvoir, was badly injured after the battle of Mount Tumbledown and had to have his left leg amputated. But since then he has excelled himself and won a host of trophies taking part in disabled sporting events. It was a few weeks after his 21st birthday in May 1982 when Robert was at Mount Tumbledown, the scene of one of the most notorious battles of the Falklands. His regiment took heavy fire and nine men were killed, with 43 wounded. Robert escaped unharmed, but while escorting injured soldiers back to a regimental aid post, he came under a mortar attack.

Two men were killed and Robert got a piece of shrapnel in his thigh.

Six days later, he was told his leg would have to be amputated "I didn't find out until I was on the operating table. They said "we need you to sign a consent form", I asked them to tell me what they were doing and I'd consent to it."

He was flown home and had an emotional reunion with his family. "It was the only time I've seen my Dad speechless. I joked with him "I've gone and put my big foot in it now." Robert had a prosthetic leg fitted and began rebuilding his life: "It was very much trial and error. I had to try one thing and if that didn't work, try another."

"At the time I simply thought: it's happened and I've just got to sort it out. Everyone deals with things in their own way, and how I coped may not necessarily work for anyone else." He threw himself into sport, taking part in everything from volleyball to field athletics.

"It was the same for me as it was for any athlete. You set yourself a target and hopefully you win. If you don't you do better next time."

Robert refuses to be bitter about his injury. He was based in London in 1992 when he received a visit from Argentine President Carlos Menem, a political prisoner at the time of the Falklands War.

"I got a bottle of wine from him and people said to me "Haven't you got a problem with that?" I said it was hardly his fault; he was in the nick while it was all happening."

"His translator told him what I said and he asked me to give back the bottle of wine. I thought I'd upset him, but he signed it and gave it back to me."

A touching moment came a few years earlier when he was at a disabled ex-service sporting tournament in Stoke Mandeville, and met an Argentine soldier. "I met his family and sat his daughter on my lap. He was in tears and his wife, who had to translate, told me he never believed in 1982 that men who tried to kill one another would be so close to each other now. When he went home his mother's neighbour, whose son was killed on Tumbledown, sent me her son's rosary which I still have."

"I met a few Argentinean solders in my time, but there was never any bad feeling. We were just doing a job, and they said to me that if we got rid of the politicians we'd be a lot better off."

Twenty five years later, he now lives in Croxton Kerrial and remains philosophical about his experience: "It's something that happened, and we were there when it did."

"If I hadn't lost my leg there, maybe it would have happened when I was crossing the road at home."

"Whatever happened to me, the fact is I'm still here. There are many who are not."

Printed in Great Britain
by Amazon

81832906R00031